Gluten-Free

SNACKS

3

What is Gluten?

Gluten is a protein that is found in wheat, rye, and barley. There are many reasons people avoid gluten. Some people are allergic to wheat itself while others may have a sensitivity to gluten and just feel better when they avoid it. The most serious is Celiac Disease, in which the body produces an autoimmune response after eating gluten. The only way to manage this condition is to follow a strict gluten-free diet.

No More Bread? No Pasta?

At first, going gluten-free may appear to be rather limiting. Fortunately, there are many more delicious foods on the gluten-free list than on the forbidden list. There are also more and more products, from cereals to baking mixes to pastas, which are now being formulated in gluten-free versions. These days you'll find them not just in health food stores and online, but also on the shelves of most major supermarkets.

Some Good News

Spotting hidden gluten in processed foods is a lot easier now thanks to the FDA's Food Allergy Labeling Law that went into effect in 2004. Since wheat is a common allergen, any product that contains wheat or is derived from it must say so on the label. That means formerly questionable ingredients, such as modified food starch or maltodextrin, must now show wheat as part of their name if they were made from it (for example, "wheat maltodextrin"). Be aware that this ONLY applies to foods produced in the US and Canada. Imports are a different matter.

More Good News

Look at your dietary restrictions as an opportunity to try new foods. Add quinoa and chickpea flour to your cupboard. Use corn tortillas to make sandwiches or lasagna. You'll find easy recipes in this book that are so delicious you'll forget that they're gluten-free. Healthy eating may actually be easier without gluten, too. Adding more fresh produce to your meals, eating less processed food and avoiding refined flour are all steps to a better diet for anyone.

Gluten-Free Flour Blends

While there are many products that are now readily available in the supermarkets, they can be rather expensive. We have provided a basic flour blend that can be prepared in bulk and kept on hand for use at any time. Please refer to this when preparing many of the recipes in this book.

Gluten-Free All-Purpose Flour Blend

- **1 cup white rice flour**
- **1 cup sorghum flour**
- **1 cup tapioca flour**
- **1 cup cornstarch**
- **1 cup almond flour or coconut flour**

Combine all ingredients in large bowl. Whisk to make sure flours are evenly distributed. The recipe can be doubled or tripled. Store in airtight container in the refrigerator.

Makes about 5 cups

Edamame Hummus

- **1 package (16 ounces) frozen shelled edamame, thawed**
- **2 green onions, coarsely chopped (about $1/2$ cup)**
- **$1/2$ cup loosely packed fresh cilantro**
- **3 to 4 tablespoons water**
- **2 tablespoons canola oil**
- **$1^1/2$ tablespoons fresh lime juice**
- **1 tablespoon honey**
- **2 cloves garlic**
- **1 teaspoon salt**
- **$1/4$ teaspoon black pepper**
- **Rice crackers and/or vegetable sticks**

1. Combine edamame, green onions, cilantro, 3 tablespoons water, oil, lime juice, honey, garlic, salt and pepper in food processor; process until smooth. Add additional water to thin dip, if necessary.

2. Serve with rice crackers and/or vegetable sticks for dipping. Store in refrigerator up to 4 days.

Makes 2 cups
(about 16 servings)

Citrus Candied Nuts

- **1 egg white**
- **$1^1/2$ cups whole almonds**
- **$1^1/2$ cups pecan halves**
- **1 cup powdered sugar**
- **2 tablespoons fresh lemon juice**
- **2 teaspoons grated orange peel**
- **1 teaspoon grated lemon peel**
- **$1/8$ teaspoon ground nutmeg**

1. Preheat oven to 300°F. Grease 15X10-inch jelly-roll pan.

2. Beat egg white in medium bowl with electric mixer at high speed until soft peaks form. Add almonds and pecans; stir until well coated. Stir in powdered sugar, lemon juice, orange peel, lemon peel and nutmeg until evenly coated. Spread nuts in single layer in prepared pan.

3. Bake 30 minutes, stirring after 20 minutes. Turn oven off. Let nuts stand in oven 15 minutes. Remove nuts from pan to sheet of foil. Cool completely. Store in airtight container up to 2 weeks.

Makes 3 cups
(about 12 servings)

Edamame Hummus

No-Bake Fruit and Grain Bars

$^1/_2$ **cup cooked amaranth**

2 **cups gluten-free whole grain puffed rice cereal**

$^1/_2$ **cup chopped dried fruits**

$^1/_2$ **cup honey**

$^1/_4$ **cup sugar**

$^3/_4$ **cup almond butter**

1. Spray 8- or 9-inch square baking pan with nonstick cooking spray.

2. Heat medium saucepan over high heat. Add 1 tablespoon amaranth; stir or gently shake saucepan until almost all seeds have popped. (Partially cover saucepan if seeds are popping over the side.) Remove to medium bowl. Repeat with remaining amaranth.

3. Stir cereal and dried fruits into popped amaranth.

4. Combine honey and sugar in same saucepan; bring to a boil over medium heat. Remove from heat; stir in almond butter until melted and smooth.

5. Pour honey mixture over cereal mixture; stir until evenly coated. Press firmly into prepared pan. Let stand until set. Cut into bars.

Makes 16 bars

Magic Rainbow Pops

1 **envelope (1/4 ounce) unflavored gelatin**

1/4 **cup cold water**

1/2 **cup boiling water**

1 **container (6 ounces) raspberry or strawberry yogurt**

1 **container (6 ounces) lemon or orange yogurt**

1 **can (8 1/4 ounces) apricots or peaches with juice**

Pop molds with lids

1. Combine gelatin and cold water in 2-cup glass measuring cup. Let stand 5 minutes to soften. Add boiling water. Stir until gelatin is completely dissolved. Cool.

2. For first layer, combine raspberry yogurt and 1/4 cup gelatin mixture in small bowl; stir until completely blended. Fill each pop mold about one third full with raspberry mixture.* Freeze 30 to 60 minutes or until set.

3. For second layer, combine lemon yogurt and 1/4 cup gelatin mixture in small bowl; stir until completely blended. Pour lemon mixture over raspberry layer in each mold.* Freeze 30 to 60 minutes or until set.

4. For third layer, combine apricots with juice and remaining 1/4 cup gelatin mixture in blender or food processor; blend until smooth. Pour mixture over lemon layer in each mold.* Cover with lids. Freeze 2 to 5 hours or until firm.**

5. To remove pops from molds, place bottoms of pops under warm running water until loosened. Press firmly on bottoms to release. (Do not twist or pull lids.)

Makes about 6 pops

Pour any extra mixture into small paper cups. Freeze as directed in the tip.

**If you aren't using pop molds with lids, cover each pop with small piece of foil and insert pop sticks through center of foil.*

Tip: Three-ounce paper or plastic cups can be used in place of the molds. Make the layers as directed or put a single flavor in each cup and cover each cup with small piece of foil and freeze 1 hour before inserting sticks. Freeze until firm. To serve, remove foil and peel away paper cups or gently twist frozen pops out of plastic cups.

Graham Crackers

- 1/2 **cup sweet rice flour (mochiko), plus additional for work surface**
- 1/2 **cup sorghum flour**
- 1/2 **cup packed brown sugar**
- 1/3 **cup tapioca flour**
- 1/2 **teaspoon baking soda**
- 1/2 **teaspoon salt**
- 1/4 **cup (1/2 stick) butter**
- 2 **tablespoons plus 2 teaspoons whole milk**
- 2 **tablespoons honey**
- 1 **tablespoon vanilla**

1. Combine 1/2 cup sweet rice flour, sorghum flour, brown sugar, tapioca flour, baking soda and salt in food processor; pulse until combined. Add butter; pulse until coarse crumbs form.

2. Whisk milk, honey and vanilla in small bowl or measuring cup until well blended and honey is dissolved. Pour into flour mixture; process until dough forms. (Dough will be very soft and sticky.)

3. Transfer dough to floured surface; pat into rectangle. Wrap in plastic wrap and refrigerate at least 4 hours or up to 2 days.

4. Preheat oven to 325°F. Cover work surface with parchment paper; generously dust with flour.

5. Roll dough to 1/8-inch-thick rectangle on parchment paper using floured rolling pin. (If dough becomes too sticky, return to refrigerator or freezer for several minutes.) Place dough on parchment paper on baking sheet. Score dough into cracker shapes (do not cut all the way through). Prick dough in rows with tines of fork. Place baking sheet in freezer 5 to 10 minutes or in refrigerator 15 to 20 minutes.

6. Bake chilled crackers 25 minutes or until firm and slightly darkened. Transfer parchment paper to wire rack to cool. Cut crackers when cooled slightly. Cool completely before serving.

Makes about 12 crackers (about 6 servings)

Serving Suggestion: Serve crackers as a snack or for s'mores with chocolate and marshmallows.

Tip: Crush extra crackers (or less than perfect ones) and use for graham cracker crumbs.

Cheddar Crackers

1$^1/_2$ **cups brown rice flour**

  1 **teaspoon garlic powder**

  1 **teaspoon salt-free Italian seasoning**

$^1/_2$ **teaspoon salt**

$^1/_2$ **cup (2 ounces) finely grated sharp Cheddar cheese**

  6 **tablespoons ($^3/_4$ stick) cold butter, cut into small pieces**

$^1/_2$ **cup cold water**

1. Combine brown rice flour, garlic powder, Italian seasoning and salt in food processor or blender; process until well blended. Add cheese and butter; pulse until coarse crumbs form. Add water; process until dough forms.

2. Divide dough into two pieces; wrap in plastic wrap and refrigerate 20 minutes.

3. Preheat oven to 350°F. Line baking sheets with parchment paper.

4. Place each dough half between two pieces of parchment paper; roll out to $^1/_{16}$-inch thickness. Refrigerate 5 minutes.

5. Cut dough into 2$^1/_2$-inch squares; place on prepared baking sheets.

6. Bake 15 minutes or until golden and crisp, rotating baking sheets after 10 minutes. Cool on baking sheets 10 minutes. Remove to wire racks; cool completely.

Makes 24 crackers (about 6 servings)

Cinnamon-Honey Pops

1¼ cups plain nonfat Greek
     yogurt

½ cup honey

¼ cup fat-free (skim) milk

1 tablespoon sugar

½ teaspoon ground cinnamon

½ teaspoon vanilla

    Pop molds or paper or
     plastic cups

    Pop sticks

1. Combine yogurt, honey, milk, sugar, cinnamon and vanilla in blender or food processor; blend until smooth.

2. Pour mixture into molds. Cover top of each mold with small piece of foil. Freeze 2 hours.*

3. Insert sticks through center of foil. Freeze 4 hours or until firm.

4. To remove pops from molds, remove foil and place bottoms of pops under warm running water until loosened. Press firmly on bottoms to release. (Do not twist or pull sticks.)

Makes 6 pops

If using pop molds with lids, skip step 3 and freeze until firm.

Asian Party Mix

3 cups gluten-free rice cereal squares

3 cups gluten-free corn cereal squares

2 cups gluten-free mini pretzels

1 cup roasted salted soynuts

1 cup dry-roasted salted peanuts

5 tablespoons unsalted butter, melted

3 tablespoons gluten-free soy sauce

2 tablespoons packed brown sugar

2 tablespoons gluten-free teriyaki sauce

$^1/_2$ teaspoon ground ginger

$^1/_2$ teaspoon garlic salt

$^1/_4$ teaspoon ground red pepper

1. Preheat oven to 250°F.

2. Combine cereals, pretzels, soynuts and peanuts in large bowl. Whisk butter, soy sauce, brown sugar, teriyaki sauce, ginger, garlic salt and ground red pepper in small bowl until smooth. Pour over cereal mixture; toss to coat evenly. Spoon mixture into 13X9-inch baking pan.

3. Bake 1 hour, stirring every 15 minutes. Spread on paper towels to cool completely. Store in airtight container.

Makes 12 cups
(about 24 servings)

Wasabi Cream Cheese Spread

8 ounces low-fat cream cheese, softened

2 tablespoons fresh lime juice

1 tablespoon prepared wasabi paste

2 teaspoons rice vinegar

2 tablespoons thawed frozen shelled edamame

2 tablespoons chopped green onion, plus additional for garnish

Rice crackers

1. Combine cream cheese, lime juice, wasabi paste and vinegar in small bowl; mix well. Fold in edamame and 2 tablespoons green onion.

2. Serve immediately or cover and refrigerate until ready to serve. Serve with rice crackers. Garnish with additional green onion.

Makes 1 cup
(about 8 servings)

Fruit Kabobs with Raspberry Yogurt Dip

1/2 cup plain nonfat yogurt

1/4 cup raspberry fruit spread

1 pint fresh strawberries

2 cups cubed honeydew melon (1-inch cubes)

2 cups cubed cantaloupe (1-inch cubes)

1 can (8 ounces) pineapple chunks in juice, drained

1. Stir yogurt and fruit spread in small bowl until well blended.

2. Thread fruit alternately onto six 12-inch skewers. Serve with yogurt dip.

Makes 6 servings

Wasabi Cream Cheese Spread

Chewy Corn Bread Cookies

1 cup (2 sticks) unsalted butter, softened

$^2/_3$ cup plus 2 tablespoons sugar, divided

1 egg

1 teaspoon vanilla

$^1/_2$ teaspoon salt

2 cups corn flour

$^1/_2$ cup instant polenta

1. Beat butter and $^2/_3$ cup sugar in large bowl with electric mixer at medium-high speed until creamy. Beat in egg, vanilla and salt until well blended. Combine corn flour and polenta in medium bowl. Gradually add to butter mixture, beating well after each addition. (Dough will be very sticky.)

2. Shape dough into two discs. Wrap in plastic wrap; refrigerate at least 2 hours.

3. Preheat oven to 350°F. Line cookie sheets with parchment paper.

4. Shape dough into 1-inch balls. Roll in remaining 2 tablespoons sugar. Place 1 inch apart on prepared cookie sheets.

5. Bake 12 to 14 minutes. Cool completely on cookie sheets.

Makes 4 dozen cookies

Polenta Pizzas

1 teaspoon olive oil

$^1/_2$ cup chopped onion

$^1/_4$ pound gluten-free bulk mild Italian sausage

1 can (8 ounces) gluten-free pizza sauce

1 roll (16 ounces) prepared polenta

1 cup (4 ounces) shredded mozzarella cheese

1. Preheat oven to 350°F. Spray 13X9-inch baking pan with nonstick cooking spray.

2. Heat oil in large nonstick skillet over medium heat. Add onion; cook and stir 3 minutes or until tender. Add sausage; cook 5 minutes or until browned, stirring to break up meat. Stir in pizza sauce; simmer 5 minutes.

3. Cut polenta roll into 16 slices; arrange in prepared pan. Spoon 1 heaping tablespoonful sausage mixture and 1 tablespoon cheese over each polenta slice.

4. Bake 15 minutes or until heated through and cheese is melted.

Makes 4 to 6 servings

Lemony Arrowroot Cookies

Cookies

- ¼ **cup (½ stick) butter**
- ⅓ **cup granulated sugar**
- 1 **egg**
- **Grated peel and juice of 1 lemon**
- ½ **teaspoon vanilla**
- 1¼ **cups Gluten-Free All-Purpose Flour Blend (page 5),* plus additional for work surface**
- ½ **cup arrowroot**
- ½ **teaspoon baking powder**
- ¼ **teaspoon salt**

Glaze

- ¼ **cup powdered sugar**
- 1 **teaspoon grated lemon peel, plus additional for garnish**
- 1 **tablespoon lemon juice, plus additional, if necessary**

*Or use any all-purpose gluten-free flour blend that does not contain xanthan gum.

1. Preheat oven to 350°F. Grease cookie sheet.

2. Beat butter and granulated sugar in large bowl with electric mixer at medium speed until creamy. Add egg, grated peel and juice of 1 lemon and vanilla; beat until well blended. Add 1¼ cups flour blend, arrowroot, baking powder and salt; beat at low speed just until combined.

3. Roll out dough onto floured surface to ⅛-inch thickness. Cut out shapes with desired cookie cutters. Place on prepared cookie sheet.

4. Bake 8 to 10 minutes. (Cookies will not brown.) Remove to wire rack; cool completely.

5. Combine powdered sugar and 1 teaspoon lemon peel in small bowl; stir in enough lemon juice to make pourable glaze. Drizzle glaze over cookies. Garnish with additional lemon peel.

Makes 1 dozen cookies

Sweet & Spicy Popcorn Clusters

¹/₂ **cup sugar**

6 **tablespoons (³/₄ stick) butter**

4 **teaspoons light corn syrup**

¹/₂ **teaspoon salt**

¹/₂ **teaspoon ground red pepper**

12 **cups popped light butter-flavored microwave popcorn**

1. Combine sugar, butter, corn syrup, salt and ground red pepper in large saucepan. Bring to a boil over medium heat; boil 3 minutes. Remove from heat.

2. Immediately stir in popcorn; toss to coat evenly.

3. Spread mixture in single layer on baking sheets. Let stand 1 hour to cool completely. Break into clusters. Store in airtight container.

Makes 6 servings

Energy Smoothie

1 **package (16 ounces) frozen unsweetened strawberries, partially thawed**

2 **bananas, sliced**

1 **container (6 ounces) vanilla nonfat Greek yogurt**

1 **cup vanilla soymilk or milk***

¹/₃ **cup powdered sugar**

2 **teaspoons vanilla**

*If using milk, add 1 to 2 tablespoons additional sugar, if desired.

1. Combine strawberries, bananas, yogurt, soymilk, powdered sugar and vanilla in blender or food processor; blend until smooth.

2. Pour into four glasses. Serve immediately.

Makes 4 (8-ounce) servings

Sweet & Spicy Popcorn Clusters

Chocolate-Almond Crispy Treats

6 cups gluten-free crisp brown rice cereal

1½ cups sliced almonds, toasted*

1 cup light corn syrup

⅓ cup almond butter

¼ cup packed brown sugar

3 tablespoons unsweetened cocoa powder

¼ teaspoon salt

1 cup semisweet chocolate chips

*To toast almonds, spread in single layer in heavy skillet. Cook over medium heat 1 to 2 minutes or until nuts are lightly browned, stirring frequently.

1. Line 13X9-inch baking pan with parchment paper. Spray with nonstick cooking spray.

2. Combine rice cereal and almonds in large bowl; set aside.

3. Combine corn syrup, almond butter, brown sugar, cocoa and salt in large saucepan. Cook and stir over medium heat 5 minutes or until mixture is smooth and just begins to boil across surface. Remove from heat.

4. Immediately stir cereal mixture into saucepan. Gently fold in chocolate chips. Press firmly into prepared pan. Let stand 1 hour or until set. Cut into bars.

Makes 24 bars